THE BACKSLIDER IN HEART

By
Charles Finney

PUBLISHED by PARABLES
Earthly Stories with a Heavenly Meaning

The Backslider in Heart
Charles Finney

Published By Parables
March, 2020

All Rights Reserved. No part of this book may be reproduced or utilized in any form or by any means, electronic or mechanical, including photocopying, recording, or by any information storage and retrieval system, without permission in writing from the author.

    ISBN 978-1-951497-36-1
    Printed in the United States of America

Readers should be aware that Internet Web sites offered as citations and/or sources for further information may have been changed or disappeared between the time this was written and the time it is read.

The Backslider in Heart

By
Charles Finney

I cannot conclude this course of lectures, without warning converts against backsliding. In discussing this subject, I will show:

I. What backsliding in heart is not.

II. What backsliding in heart is.

III. What are evidences of backsliding in heart.

IV. What are consequences of backsliding in heart.

V. How to recover from this state.

1. It does not consist in the subsidence of highly excited religious emotions. The subsidence of religious feeling may be an evidence of a backslidden heart, but it does not consist in the cooling off of religious feeling.

   1. It consists in taking back that consecration to God and His service, that constitutes true conversion.

   2. It is the leaving, by a Christian, of his first love.

   3. It consists in the Christian withdrawing himself from that state of entire and universal devotion to God, which constitutes true religion, and coming again under the control of a self-pleasing spirit.

   4. The text implies that there may be a backslidden heart, when the forms of religion

and obedience to God are maintained. As we know from consciousness that men perform the same, or similar, acts from widely different, and often from opposite, motives, we are certain that men may keep up all the outward forms and appearances of religion, when in fact, they are backslidden in heart. No doubt the most intense selfishness often takes on a religious type, and there are many considerations that might lead a backslider in heart to keep up the forms, while he had lost the power of godliness in his soul.

--- ooo ---

1. Manifest formality in religious exercises. A stereotyped, formal way of saying and doing things, that is clearly the result of habit, rather than the outgushing of the religious life. This formality will be emotionless and cold as an iceberg, and will evince a total want of earnestness in the performance of religious duty. In prayer and in religious exercises the backslider in heart will pray or praise, or confess, or give thanks with his lips, so that all can hear him, perhaps, but in such a way that no one

can feel him. Such a formality would be impossible where there existed a present, living faith and love, and religious zeal.

2. A lack of religious enjoyment is evidence of a backslidden heart. We always enjoy the saying and doing of those things that please those whom we most love; furthermore, when the heart is not backslidden, communion with God is kept up, and therefore all religious duties are not only performed with pleasure, but the communion with God involved in them is a source of rich and continual enjoyment. If we do not enjoy the service of God, it is because we do not truly serve Him. If we love Him supremely, it is impossible that we should not enjoy His service at every step. Always remember then, whenever you lose your religious enjoyment, or the enjoyment of serving God, you may know that you are not serving Him aright.

3. Religious bondage is another evidence of a backslidden heart. God has no slaves. He does not accept the service of bondsmen, who serve Him because they must. He accepts none but a love service. A backslider in heart finds his religious

duties a burden to him. He has promised to serve the Lord. He dare not wholly break off from the form of service, and he tries to be dutiful, while he has no heart in prayer, in praise, in worship, or in any of those exercises which are so spontaneous and delightful, where there is true love to God. The backslider in heart is often like a dutiful, but unloving wife. She tries to do her duty to her husband, but fails utterly because she does not love him. Her painstaking to please her husband is constrained, not the spontaneous outburst of a loving heart; and her relationship and her duties become the burden of her life. She goes about complaining of the weight of care that is upon her, and will not be likely to advise young ladies to marry. She is committed for life, and must therefore perform the duties of married life, but it is such a bondage! Just so with religious bondage. The professor must perform his duty. He drags painfully about it, and you will hear him naturally sing backslider's hymns:

Reason I hear, her counsels weigh,
And all her words approve
And yet I find it hard to obey,
And harder still, to love.

4. An ungoverned temper. While the heart is full of love, the temper will naturally be chastened and sweet, or at any rate, the will keep it under, and not suffer it to break out in outrageous abuse, or if at any time it should so far escape from the control of the will as to break loose in hateful words, it will soon be brought under, and by no means
suffered to take control and manifest itself to the annoyance of others. Especially will a loving heart confess and break down, if at any time bad temper gets the control. Whenever, therefore, there is an irritable, uncontrolled temper allowed to manifest itself to those around, you may know there is a backslidden heart.

5. A spirit of uncharitableness is evidence of a backslidden heart. By this, I mean a lack of that disposition that puts the best construction upon every one's conduct that can be reasonable a lack of confidence in the good intentions and professions of others. We naturally credit the good professions of those whom we love. We naturally attribute to them right motives, and put the best allowable construction upon their words and deeds. Where

there is a lack of this there is evidence conclusive of a backslidden or unloving heart.

6. A censorious spirit is conclusive evidence of a backslidden heart. This is a spirit of fault-finding, of impugning the motives of others, when their conduct admits of a charitable construction. It is a disposition to fasten blame upon others, and judge them harshly. It is a spirit of distrust of Christian character and profession. It is a state of mind that reveals itself in harsh judgments, harsh sayings, and the manifestation of uncomfortable feelings toward individuals. This state of mind is entirely incompatible with a loving heart, and whenever a censorious spirit is manifested by a professor of religion, you may know there is a backslidden heart.

7. A lack of interest in God's Word, is also an evidence of a backslidden heart. Perhaps nothing more conclusively proves that a professor has a backslidden heart, than his losing his interest in the Bible. While the heart is full of love, no book in the world is so precious as the Bible. But when the love is gone, the Bible becomes not only uninteresting but often repulsive. There is no faith to accept its

promises, but conviction enough left to dread its threatening. But in general the backslider in heart is apathetic as to the Bible. He does not read it much, and when he does read it, he has not interest enough to understand it. Its pages become dark and uninteresting, and therefore it is neglected.

8. A lack of interest in secret prayer is also an evidence of a backslidden heart. Young Christian, if you find yourself losing your interest in the Bible and in secret prayer, stop short, return to God, and give yourself no rest, till you enjoy the light of His countenance. If you feel disinclined to pray, or to read your Bible; if when you pray and read your Bible, you have no heart; if you are inclined to make your secret devotions short, or are easily induced to neglect them; or if your thoughts, affections, and emotions wander, you may know that you are a backslider in heart, and your first business is to be broken down before God, and to see that your love and zeal are renewed.

9. A lack of interest in the conversion of souls and in efforts to promote revivals of religion. This of course reveals a backslidden heart. There is nothing in

which a loving heart takes more interest than in the conversion of souls in revivals of religion, and in efforts to promote them.

10. A lack of interest in published accounts or narratives of revivals of religion, is also an evidence of a backslidden heart. While one retains his interest in the conversion of souls, and in revivals of religion he will, of course, be interested in all accounts of revivals of religion anywhere. If you find yourself, therefore, disinclined to read such accounts, or find yourself not interested in them, take it for granted that you are backslidden in heart.

11. The same is true of missions, and missionary work and operations. If you lose your interest in the work, and in the conversion of the heathen, and do not delight to read and hear of the success of missions, you may know that you are backslidden in heart.

12. The loss of interest in benevolent enterprises generally is an evidence of a backslidden heart. I say, "the loss of interest," for surely, if you were ever converted to Christ, you have had an interest

in all benevolent enterprises that came within your knowledge. Religion consists in disinterested benevolence. Of course, a converted soul takes the deepest interest in all benevolent efforts to reform and save mankind; in good government, in Christian education, in the cause of temperance, in the abolition of slavery, in provision for the needs of the poor, and in short, in every good word and work. Just in proportion as you have lost your interest in these, you have evidence that you are backslidden in heart.

13. The loss of interest in truly spiritual conversation is another evidence of a backslidden heart. "Out of the abundance of the heart the mouth speaketh" (Matthew 12:34). This our Lord Jesus Christ announced as a law of our nature. No conversation is so sweet to a truly loving heart, as that which relates to Christ, and to our living Christian experience. If you find yourself losing interest in conversing on heart religion, and of the various and wonderful experiences of Christians, if you have known what the true love of God is, you have fallen from it, and are a backslider in heart.

14. A loss of interest in the conversation and society of highly spiritual people, is an evidence of a backslidden heart. We take the greatest delight in the society of those who are most interested in the things that are most dear to us.

Hence, a loving Christian heart will always seek the society of those who are most spiritually minded, and whose conversation is most evangelical and spiritual. If you find yourself wanting in this respect, then know for certain that you are backslidden in heart.

15. The loss of interest in the question of sanctification is an evidence of a backslidden heart. I say again, the loss of interest, for, if you ever truly knew the love of God, you must have had a great interest in the question of entire consecration to God, or of entire sanctification. If you are a Christian, you have felt that sin was an abomination to your soul. You have had inexpressible longings to be rid of it forever, and everything that could throw light upon that question

of agonizing importance was most intensely interesting to you. If this question has been dismissed, and you no longer take an interest in it, it is because you are backslidden in heart.

16. The loss of interest in those newly converted, is also an evidence of a backslidden heart. The Psalmist says: "They that fear Thee will be glad when they see me; because I have hoped in Thy word" (Psalm 119:74). This he puts into the mouth of a convert, and who does not know that this is true? There is joy in the presence of the angels of God, over one sinner that repenteth, and is there not joy among the saints on earth, over those that come to Christ, and are as babes newly born into the Kingdom? Show me a professor of religion who does not manifest an absorbing interest in converts to Christ, and I will show you a backslider in heart, and a hypocrite; he professes religion, but has none.

17. An uncharitable state of mind in regard to professed converts, is also an evidence of a backslidden heart. Charity, or love, "believeth all things, hopeth all things" (1 Corinthians 13:7), is

very ready to judge kindly and favorably of those who profess to be converted to Christ, and will naturally watch over them with interest, pray for them, instruct them, and have as much confidence in them as it is reasonable to have. A disposition, therefore, to pick at, criticize, and censure them, is an evidence of a backslidden heart.

18. The lack of the spirit of prayer is evidence of a backslidden heart. While the love of Christ remains fresh in the soul, the indwelling Spirit of God will reveal Himself as the Spirit of grace and supplication. He will beget strong desires in the soul for the salvation of sinners and the sanctification of saints. He will often make intercessions in them, with great longings, strong crying and tears, and with groanings that cannot he uttered in words, for those things that are according to the will of God. Or, to express it in Scripture language, according to Paul: "Likewise the Spirit also helpeth our infirmities: for we know not what we should pray for as we ought: but the Spirit itself maketh intercession for us with groanings which cannot be uttered. And He that searcheth the hearts knoweth what is the mind of the Spirit, because He maketh intercession

for the saints according to the will of God" (Romans 8:26, 27). If the spirit of prayer departs, it is a sure indication of a backslidden heart, for while the first love of a Christian continues he is sure to be drawn by the Holy Spirit to wrestle much in prayer.

19. A backslidden heart often reveals itself by the manner in which people pray. For example, praying as if in a state of self-condemnation, or very much like a convicted sinner, is an evidence of a backslidden heart. Such a person will reveal the fact, that he is not at peace with God. His confessions and self-accusations will show to others what perhaps he does not well understand himself. His manner of praying will reveal the fact that he has not communion with God; that instead of being filled with faith and love, he is more or less convicted of sin, and conscious that he is not in a state of acceptance with God. He will naturally pray more like a convicted sinner than like a Christian. It will be seen by his prayer that he is not in a state of Christian liberty that he is having a Seventh of Romans experience, instead of that which is described in the Eighth.

20. A backslidden heart will further reveal itself in praying almost exclusively for self, and for those friends that are regarded almost as parts of self. It is often very striking and even shocking to attend a backsliders' prayer meeting, and I am very sorry to say that many prayer meetings of the Church are little else. Their prayers are timid and hesitating, and reveal the fact that they have little or no faith. Instead of surrounding the Throne of Grace and pouring their hearts out for a blessing on those around them, they have to be urged up to duty, to "take up their cross." Their hearts do not, will not, spontaneously gush out to God in prayer. They have very little concern for others, and when they do, as they say, "take up their cross and do their duty," and pretend to lead in prayer, it will be observed that they pray just like a company of convicted sinners, almost altogether for themselves. They will pray for that which, should they obtain it, would be religion, just as a convicted sinner would pray for a new heart; and the fact that they pray for religion as they do, manifests that they have none, in their present state of mind. Ask them to pray for the conversion of sinners, and they will either wholly forget to do so, or just mention sinners in such a

way as will show that they have no heart to pray for them.

I have known professed Christian parents to get into such a state that they had no heart to pray for the conversion of their own children, even when those children were under conviction. They would keep up family prayer, and attend a weekly prayer meeting, but would never get out of the rut of praying round and round for themselves. A few years since I was laboring in a revival in a Presbyterian Church. At the close of the evening sermon I found that the daughter of one of the elders of the Church was in great distress of mind. I observed that her convictions were very deep. We had been holding a meeting with inquirers in the vestry, and I had just dismissed the inquirers, when this young lady came to me in great agitation and begged me to pray for her. The people had mostly gone, except a few who were waiting in the body of the church for those friends who had attended the meeting of inquiry. I called the father of this young lady into the vestry that he might see the very anxious state of his daughter's mind. After a short personal conversation with her in the presence of her father, I called on him to pray for her, and said that I would follow him, and I urged her to give her heart to Christ. We all knelt, and he went through with his prayer, kneeling by the side of his sobbing daughter, without ever mentioning her case. His prayer revealed that he had no more religion than she had, and that he was very much in her state of mind under an awful sense of condemnation. He had kept up the appearance of religion. As an elder of the Church, he was obliged to keep up appearances. He had gone round and round upon the treadmill of his duties, while his heart was utterly backslidden. It is often almost nauseating to attend a prayer meeting of the backslidden in heart. They will go round, round, one after the other, in reality praying for their own conversion. They do not so express it, but that is the real import of their prayer. They could not render it more evident that they are backsliders in heart.

21. Absence from stated prayer meetings for slight reasons, is a sure indication of a backslidden heart. No meeting is more interesting to Christians than the prayer meeting, and while they have any heart to pray, they will not be absent from prayer meeting

unless prevented from attending by the providence of God. If a call from a friend at the hour of meeting can prevent their attendance, unless the call is made under very peculiar circumstances, it is strong evidence that they do not wish to attend, and hence, that they are backsliders in heart. A call at such a time would not prevent their attending a wedding, a party, a picnic, or an amusing lecture. The fact is, it is hypocrisy for them to pretend that they really want to go, while they can be kept away for slight reasons.

22. The same is true of the neglect of family prayer, for slight reasons. While the heart is engaged in religion, Christians will not readily omit family devotions, and whenever they are ready to find an excuse for the omission, it is a sure evidence that they are backslidden in heart.

23. When secret prayer is regarded more as a duty than as a privilege, it is because the heart is backslidden. It has always appeared to me almost ridiculous, to hear Christians speak of prayer as a "duty." It is one of the greatest of earthly privileges. What should we think of a child coming to its parent

for its dinner, not because it is hungry, but as a duty. How would it strike us to hear a beggar speak of the "duty" of asking alms of us. It is an infinite privilege to be allowed to come to God, and ask for the supply of all our wants. But to pray because we must, rather than because we may, seems unnatural. To ask for what we want, and because we want it, and because God has encouraged us to ask, and has promised to answer our request, is natural and reasonable. But to pray as a duty and as if we were obliging God by our prayer, is quite ridiculous, and is a certain indication of a backslidden heart.

24. Pleading for worldly amusements is also an indication of a backslidden heart. The most grateful amusements possible, to a truly spiritual mind, are those engagements that bring the soul into the most direct communion with God. While the heart is full of love and faith, an hour, or an evening, spent alone in communion with God, is more delightful than all the amusements which the world can offer. A loving heart is jealous of everything that will break up or interfere with its communion with God. For mere worldly amusements it has no relish. When the soul

does not find more delight in God than in all worldly things, the heart is sadly backslidden.

25. Spiritual blindness is another evidence of a backslidden heart. While the eye is single the whole body will be full of spiritual light, but if the eye be evil (which means a backslidden heart) the whole body will be full of darkness.

Spiritual blindness reveals itself in a lack of interest in God's Word, and in religious truth generally. It will also manifest a lack of spiritual discrimination, and will be easily imposed upon by the insinuations of Satan. A backslidden heart will lead to the adoption of lax principles of morality. It does not discern the spirituality of God's law, and of His requirements generally. When this spiritual blindness is manifest it is a sure indication that the heart is backslidden.

26. Religious apathy, with worldly wakefulness and sensibility, is a sure indication of a backslidden heart. We sometimes see persons who feel deeply and quickly on worldly subjects, but who cannot be made to feel deeply on religious subjects. This clearly indicates a backslidden state of mind.

27. A self-indulgent spirit is a sure indication of a backslidden heart. By self-indulgence, I mean a disposition to gratify the appetites, passions, and propensities, to "fulfill the desires of the
flesh and of the mind" (Ephesians 2:3).

This, in the Bible, is represented as a state of spiritual death. I am satisfied that the most common occasion of backsliding in heart is to be found in the clamor for indulgence of the various appetites and propensities. The appetite for food is frequently, and perhaps more frequently than any other, the occasion of backsliding. Few Christians, I fear, apprehend any danger in this direction. God's injunction is: "Whether therefore ye eat, or drink, or whatsoever ye do, do all to the glory of God" (1 Corinthians 10:31). Christians forget this, and eat
and drink to please themselves, consulting their appetites instead of the laws of life and health. More persons are ensnared by their tables than the Church is aware of. The table is a snare of death to multitudes that no man can number. A great many people who avoid alcoholic drinks altogether, will indulge in tea and coffee, and even tobacco, and in food that, both in quantity and quality, violates every

law of health. They seem to have no other law than that of appetite, and this they so deprave by abuse that, to indulge it, is to ruin body nd soul together. Show me a gluttonous professor, and I will show you a backslider.

28. A seared conscience is also an evidence of a backslidden heart. While the soul is wakeful and loving, the conscience is as tender as the apple of the eye. But when the heart is backslidden, the conscience is silent and seared, on many subjects. Such a person will tell you that he is not violating his conscience, in eating or drinking, or in self-indulgence of any kind. You will find a backslider has but little conscience. The same will very generally be true in regard to sins of omission. Multitudes of duties may be neglected and a seared conscience will remain silent. Where conscience is not awake, the heart is surely backslidden.

29. Loose moral principles are a sure indication of a backslidden heart. A backslider in heart will write letters on the Sabbath, engage in secular reading, and in much worldly conversation. In business, such

a person will take little advantages, play off business tricks, and conform to the habits of worldly business men in the transaction of business; he will be guilty of deception and misrepresentation in making bargains, will demand exorbitant interest, and take advantage of the necessities of his fellow-men.

30. Prevalence of the fear of man is an evidence of a backslidden heart. While the heart is full of the love of God, God is feared, and not man. A desire for the applause of men is kept down, and it is enough to please God, whether men are pleased or displeased. But when the love of God is abated, "the fear of man," that "bringeth a snare" (Proverbs 29:25), gets possession of the backslider. To please man rather than God, is then his aim. In such a state he will sooner offend
God than man.

31. A sticklishness about forms, ceremonies, and nonessentials, gives evidence of a backslidden heart. A loving heart is particular only about the substance and power of religion, and will not stickle about its forms.

32. A captiousness about measures in promoting revivals of religion, is a sure evidence of a backslidden heart. Where the heart is fully set upon the conversion of sinners and the sanctification of believers, it will naturally approach the subject in the most direct manner, and by means in the highest degree calculated to accomplish the end. It will not object to, nor stumble at, measures that are evidently blessed of God, but will exert the utmost sagacity in devising the most suitable means to accomplish the great end on which the heart is set.

-- 000 ---

The text says, that "the backslider in heart shall be filled with his own ways."

1. He shall be filled with his own works. But these are dead works, they are not works of faith and love, which are acceptable to God, but are the filthy rags of his own righteousness. If they are performed as religious services, they are but loathsome hypocrisy, and an abomination to God; there is no heart in them. To such a person God says: "Who hath required this at your hand?" (Isaiah 1:12). "Ye

are they which justify yourselves before men; but God knoweth your hearts: for that which is highly esteemed among men is abomination in the sight of God" (Luke 16:15). "I know you, that ye have not the love of God in you" (John 5:42).

2. He shall be filled with his own feelings. Instead of that sweet peace and rest, and joy in the Holy Ghost, that he once experienced, he will find himself in a state of unrest, dissatisfied with himself and everybody else, his feelings often painful, humiliating, and as unpleasant and unlovely as can be well conceived. It is often very trying to live with backsliders. They are often peevish, censorious, and irritating, in all their ways. They have forsaken God, and in their feelings there is more of hell than of heaven.

3. They will be filled with their own prejudices. Their willingness to know and do the truth has gone. They will very naturally commit themselves against any truth that bears hardly upon a self-indulgent spirit. They will endeavor to justify themselves, will neither read nor hear that which will rebuke their backslidden state, and they will become deeply

prejudiced against every one that shall cross their path, who shall reprove them, accounting him as an enemy. They hedge themselves in, and shut their eyes against the light; stand on the defensive, and criticize everything that would search them out.

4. A backslider in heart will be filled with his own enmities. He will chafe in almost every relation of life, will allow himself to be vexed, and to get into such relations with some persons, and perhaps with many, that he cannot pray for them honestly, and can hardly treat them with common civility. This is an almost certain result of a backslidden heart.

5. The backslider in heart will be full of his own mistakes. He is not walking with God. He has fallen out of the Divine order. He is not led by the Spirit, but is walking in spiritual darkness. In this state he is sure to fall into many and grievous mistakes, and may get entangled in such a way as to mar his happiness, and, perhaps, destroy his usefulness for life. Mistakes in business, mistakes in forming new relations in life, mistakes in using his time, his tongue, his money, his influence; indeed, all will go

wrong with him as long as he remains in a backslidden state.

6. The backslider in heart will be filled with his own lustings. His appetites and passions, which had been kept under, have now resumed their control, and having been so long suppressed, they will seem to avenge themselves by becoming more clamorous and despotic than ever. The animal appetites and passions will burst forth, to the astonishment of the backslider, and he will probably find himself more under their influence and more enslaved by them than ever before.

7. The backslider in heart will be filled with his own words. While in that state, he will not, and cannot, control his tongue. It will prove itself to be an unruly member, full of deadly poison. By his words he will involve himself in many difficulties and perplexities, from which he can never extricate himself until he comes back to God.

8. He will be full of his own trials. Instead of keeping out of temptation, he will run right into it. He will bring upon himself multitudes of trials that he never

would have had, had he not departed from God. He will complain of his trials, but yet will constantly multiply them. A backslider feels his trials keenly, but, while he complains of being so tried by everything around him, he is constantly aggravating them, and, being the author of them, he seems industrious to bring them upon himself like an avalanche.

9. The backslider in heart shall be full of his own folly. Having rejected the Divine guidance, he will evidently fall into the depths of his own foolishness. He will inevitably say and do multitudes of foolish and ridiculous things. Being a professor of religion, these things will be all the more noticed, and of course bring him all the more into ridicule and contempt. A backslider is, indeed, the most foolish person in the world. Having experimental knowledge of the true way of life, he has the infinite folly to abandon it. Knowing the fountain of living waters, he has forsaken it, and "hewed out to himself cisterns, broken cisterns, that can hold no water" (Jeremiah 2:13). Having been guilty of this infinite folly, the whole course of his backslidden life must be that of a fool, in the Bible sense of the term.

10. The backslider in heart will be full of his own troubles. God is against him, and he is against himself. He is not at peace with God, with himself, with the Church, nor with the world. He has no inward rest. Conscience condemns him.

God condemns him. All that know his state condemn him. "There is no peace, saith my God, to the wicked" (Isaiah 57:21). There is no position in time or space in which he can be at rest.

11. The backslider in heart will be full of his own cares. He has turned back to selfishness. He counts himself and his possessions as his own. He has everything to care for. He will not hold himself and his possessions as belonging to God, and lay aside the responsibility of taking care of himself and all that he possesses. He does not, will not, cast his cares upon the Lord, but undertakes to manage everything for himself, and in his own wisdom, and for his own ends. Consequently, his cares will be multiplied, and come upon him like a deluge.

12. The backslider in heart will be full of his own perplexities. Having forsaken God, having fallen into

the darkness of his own folly, he will be filled with perplexities and doubts in regard to what course he shall pursue to accomplish his selfish ends. He is not walking with, but contrary to God. Hence, the providence of God will constantly cross his path, and baffle all his schemes. God will frown darkness upon his path, and take pains to confound his projects, and blow his schemes to the winds.

13. The backslider in heart will be filled with his own anxieties. He will be anxious about himself, about his business, about his reputation, about everything. He has taken all these things out of the hands of God, and claims them and treats them as his own. Hence, having faith in God no longer, and being unable to control events, he must of necessity be filled with anxieties with regard to the future. These anxieties are the inevitable result of his madness and folly in forsaking God.

14. The backslider in heart will be filled with his own disappointments. Having forsaken God, and taken the attitude of self-will, God will inevitably disappoint him as he pursues his selfish ends. He will frame his ways to please himself, without consulting God.

Of course God will frame his ways so as to disappoint him. Determined to have his own way, he will be greatly disappointed if his plans are frustrated; yet the certain course of events under the government of God must of necessity bring him a series of disappointments.

15. The backslider in heart must be full of his own losses. He regards his possessions as his own, his time as his own, his influence as his own, his reputation as his own. The loss of any of these, he accounts as his own loss. Having forsaken God, and being unable to control the events upon which the continuance of those things is conditioned, he will find himself suffering losses on every side. He loses his peace. He loses his property.

He loses much of his time. He loses his Christian reputation. He loses his Christian influence, and if he persists he loses his soul.

16. The backslider in heart will be full of his own crosses. All religious duty will be irksome, and, therefore, a cross to him. His state of mind will make multitudes of things crosses that in a Christian

state of mind would have been pleasant in a high degree. Having lost all heart in religion, the performance of all religious duty is a cross to his feelings. There is no help for him, unless he returns to God. The whole course of Divine providence will run across his path, and his whole life will be a series of crosses and trials. He cannot have his own way. He cannot gratify himself by accomplishing his own wishes and desires. He may beat and dash himself against the everlasting rocks of God's will and God's way, but break through and carry all before him he cannot. He must be crossed and recrossed, and crossed again, until he will fall into the Divine order, and sink into the will of God.

17. The backslider in heart will be filled with his own tempers. Having forsaken God, he will be sure to have much to irritate him. In a backslidden state, he cannot possess his soul in patience. The vexations of his backslidden life will make him nervous and irritable; his temper will become explosive and uncontrollable.

18. The backslider in heart will be full of his own disgraces. He is a rofessor of religion. The eyes of

the world are upon him, and all his inconsistencies, worldly-mindedness, follies, bad tempers, and hateful words and deeds, disgrace him in the estimation of all men who know him.

19. The backslider in heart will be full of his own delusions. Having an evil eye, his whole body will be full of darkness. He will almost certainly fall into delusions in regard to doctrines and in regard to practices. Wandering on in darkness, as he does, he will, very likely, swallow the grossest delusions. Spiritism, Mormonism, Universalism, and every other ism that is wide from the truth, will be very likely to gain possession of him. Who has not observed this of backsliders in heart?

20. The backslider in heart will be filled with his own bondage. His profession of religion brings him into bondage to the Church. He has no heart to consult the interests of the Church, or to labor for its up-building, and yet he is under covenant obligation to do so, and his reputation is at stake. He must do something to sustain religious institutions, but to do so is a bondage. If he does it, it is because he must, and not because he may. Again, he is in bondage to

God. If he performs any duty that he calls religious, it is rather as a slave than as a freeman. He serves from fear or hope, just like a slave, and not from love. A gain, he is in bondage to his own conscience. To avoid conviction and remorse, he will do or omit many things, but it is all with reluctance, and not at all of his own cordial goodwill.

21. The backslider in heart is full of his own self condemnation. Having enjoyed the love of God, and forsaken Him, he feels condemned for everything. If he attempts religious duty, he knows there is no heart in it, and hence condemns himself. If he neglects religious duty, he of course condemns himself. If he reads his Bible, it condemns him. If he does not read it, he feels condemned. If he goes to religious meetings, they condemn him; and if he stays away, he is condemned also. If he prays in secret, in his family, or in public, he knows he is not sincere, and feels condemned. If he neglects or refuses to pray, he feels condemned. Everything condemns him. His conscience is up in arms against him, and the thunders and lightnings of condemnation follow him, whithersoever he goes.

The Backslider in Heart

— ooo ---

1. Remember whence you are fallen. Take up the question at once, and deliberately contrast your present state with that in which you walked with God.

2. Take home the conviction of your true position. No longer delay to understand the exact situation between God and your soul.

3. Repent at once, and do your first works over again.

4. Do not attempt to get back, by reforming your mere outside conduct. Begin with your heart, and at once set yourself right with God.

5. Do not act like a more convicted sinner, and attempt to recommend yourself to God by any impenitent works or prayers.

Do not think that you must "reform, and make yourself better" before you can come to Christ, but understand distinctly, that coming to Christ, alone, can make you better. However much distressed you may feel, know for a certainty that until you repent and accept His will, unconditionally, you are no better, but are constantly growing worse. Until you throw yourself upon His sovereign mercy, and thus return to God, He will accept nothing at your hands.

6. Do not imagine yourself to be in a justified state, for you know you are not. Your conscience condemns you, and you know that God ought to condemn you, and if He justified you in your present state, your conscience could not justify Him. Come, then, to Christ at once, like a guilty, condemned sinner, as you are; own up, and take all the shame and blame to yourself, and believe that notwithstanding all your wanderings from God, He loves you still--that He has loved you with an everlasting love, and, therefore, with lovingkindness is drawing you.

Indexes

Index of Scripture References

Psalms

[1]119:74

Proverbs

[2]29:25

Isaiah

[3]1:12 [4]57:21

Jeremiah

[5]2:13

Matthew

[6]12:34

Luke

[7]16:15

John

[8]5:42

Romans

[9]8:26   [10]8:27

1 Corinthians

[11]10:31   [12]13:7

Ephesians

[13]2:3

-- 000 ---

Pathways To The Past

Each volume stands alone as an Individual Book
Each volume stands together with others
to enhance the value of your collection

Build your Personal, Pastoral or Church Library
Pathways To The Past contains an ever-expanding list of
Christendom's most influential authors

Augustine of Hippo
Athanasius
E. M. Bounds
John Bunyan
Robert Lewis Darby
Brother Lawrence
Jessie Penn-Lewis
Bernard of Clairvaux
Andrew Murray
Watchman Nee
Arthur W. Pink
Thomas Watson
Hannah Whitall Smith
R. A. Torrey
A. W. Tozer
Jean-Pierre de Caussade
And many, many more.

Charles Finney

The Backslider in Heart

Charles Finney

The Backslider in Heart

Charles Finney